I Get My Best Ideas by Not Thinking

Poetry by James A. Fulton

RoseDog Books
PITTSBURGH, PENNSYLVANIA 15238

RoseDog Books
585 Alpha Drive
Suite 103
Pittsburgh, PA 15238
Visit our website at *www.rosedogbookstore.com*

ISBN: 979-8-88729-110-9
eISBN: 979-8-88729-610-4

To those who came before us ....

.... and left us far too soon.

Contents

The Absent Mind

It seems I get my best ideas
When not thinking at all.
Inspiration finds me — out
Of nowhere comes the call.

My memory is average,
But I have an absent mind.
My thoughts are not from outer
Space, and surely not divine.

At times when I just take a walk,
Odd notions fill my brain.
If fortunate, I realize
I should come in from the rain.

Orphan

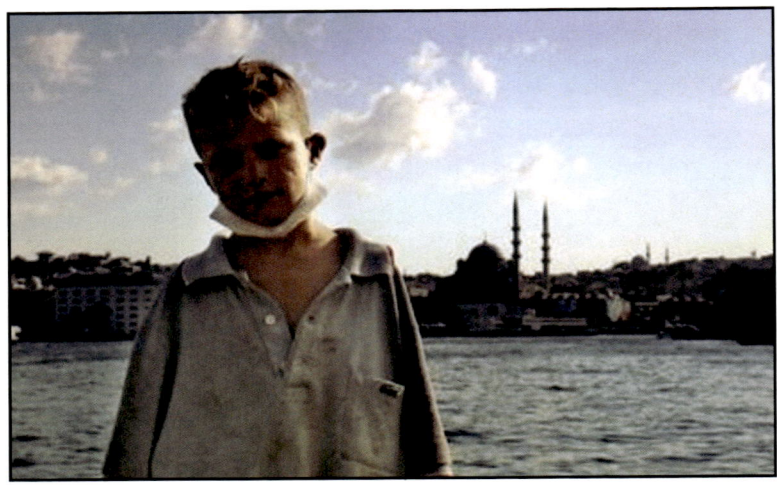

He grew up an orphan child there without choice,
His pleas and petitions not given a voice,
With so many reasons then not to rejoice,
This boy, he made do.

For so many nights he was hungry and cold,
Wondering if he would ever grow old,
All of his dreams he had just put on hold,
This boy, he made do.

Despite all the odds, he became quite a man,
And soon was applauded all over the land;
To all those who suffered he lent a strong hand,
This boy, he made do.

The Grand Opening

The patient's operation had been scheduled —
In the operating theatre for tonight.
Professors from the med school were attending;
The surgeon was extremely erudite.

Because the patient never had been starring
In theatrical performances before,
He printed invitations with engraving,
That nobody receiving could ignore:

"You are cordially invited to be present
At the following event tonight at seven:
The Opening of Wilbur Glica's Colon,
Which will Close About a Quarter to Eleven."

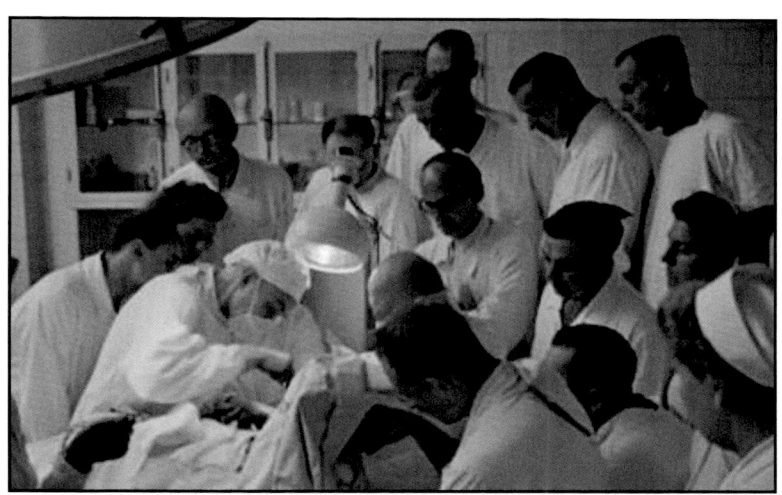

The Wreck of the Pendleton

Hard and snowy weather struck in 1952,
And tankers out at sea were not in sight.
The Pendleton was split in half by pounding ocean waves;
Eight widows, it is said, were made that night.

Other vessels in the storm sent out an S-O-S,
And Chatham Lifeboat Station heard the call.
Officers in charge sought out the bravest who were up
For taking on a savage ocean brawl.

Livesey, Maske and Webber were the seamen who agreed
To risk the ocean waves that windy day;
Engineman Fitzgerald volunteered to join the three,
To see what Father Neptune had to say.

Once out in the rescue boat, they soon were being tossed
By brutal swells that worsened by the hour.
Soon enough the Pendleton, or part of it, was seen,
And those among its crew were looking dour.

Thirty-two survivors fit on board the tiny craft —
It's still perplexing to a normal mind.
This courageous crew of four would find a way, and then
Refuse to leave a single man behind.

The Gift

The truth is a present that some won't unwrap,
For fear of what might be inside;
Once it's revealed, like what's read on a map,
The gift will forever abide.

For some, when it's known, it can be so galvanic;
For others — an obstacle stout;
But one thing is clear when the truth is titanic —
It never leaves any in doubt.

For those who may yearn to take hold of the reins
Of lives now with no looking back,
The gift they receive may cause nothing but pain —
The brave will attest to this fact.

The Last Firefly

We used to catch fireflies there in a jar,
Knowing they'd traveled from places afar,

Wait 'til the jar was a lamp all aglow,
And watch them all flash before letting them go.

Then just like a flamethrower shooting across
The lawns in the dark, we would see them get lost,

Just then I looked down at the end of my sleeve;
I noticed one who, nonetheless, wouldn't leave.

I saw in him much of myself, and I thought,
Despite how it seemed, I had never been caught.

It wasn't from lacking desire to grow;
The truth is, I really had no place to go.

Dog Walker

The dog walker had a great talent;
He didn't fear barking or growls.
He mastered the science
Of all furry clients,
And coaxed them to empty their bowels.

"That's Not Good"

She would sit there by the window,
Watch the people passing by,
And observe the action of the neighborhood.

She would see the acts of many
Friends and families she knew,
And she'd shake her head and mutter, "That's not good."

She would watch the television,
Taking in the evening news,
Tuning in a cable channel if she could.

She would never have discussion
Or express her private views,
But she'd shake her head and mutter, "That's not good."

While humanity was passing
In the long parade of life,
She'd surprise us with the things she understood.

Though she lived life in the shadows,
Her opinions were revealed
When she shook her head and muttered, "That's not good."

A Christmas Dental Emergency

Old Santa left the Arctic after dark on Christmas Eve.
He visited a billion homes, but still would never leave
A single one without a snack of milk and cookies there —
The ones left by the children with such warmth and loving care.

And when he'd almost finished yet another Christmas run,
He made it to Johannesburg before the rising sun;
And sampling a cookie that was harder than a stone,
Quite suddenly his tooth broke right beneath the buccal bone.

This man had seen the world more times than anyone around,
But still he had no clue where dental care could now be found.
'Til memories from history books returned and left him hopin'—
The stations in Antarctica were manned and always open!

Then Santa turned his sleigh 'round toward the southern continent,
So Rudolph and his nose would know exactly what he meant.
A research base was there toward which the reindeer all could head
They landed at the base and got the dentist out of bed.

And luckily, he fixed the old man's tooth without a hitch,
Then when the word got out his dental practice grew quite rich;
And had it never been for one extremely painful molar,
Old Santa would have missed the chance to say he was bipolar.

To No One

Possessing more beauty than others can boast,
She understands solitude better than most.
She waits now in vain for return of a ghost,
And she writes tender letters – to no one.

Since coming and making their only home here,
She's followed the same vigil year after year.
He's never come back, she's cried many a tear,
And she whispers her secrets – to no one.

She plays haunting melodies on her guitar,
And longingly looks at horizons afar;
Then late every night she will wish on a star,
And she sings wistful love songs – to no one.

If "The Raven" had been
Written by Dr. Seuss

A midnight so dreary left me feeling weary
While tired and bored of some unrecalled lore;
Then quick gentle tapping roused me from my napping,
When finally rapping at my chamber door.

I opened the shutter and what did I smell?
A massive supply of some guano from hell.
Right there on my bust of the mythical Pallas
Was an ebony bird who had flown in from Dallas.

And now the bird wasn't just leaving his droppings;
That bird was now talking, and he wasn't stopping —
"The bust that is here makes a wonderful perch;
It beats any pole or the top of a church."

I looked at the bust that demanded a cleaning,
And hoped that this black bird would shortly be leaving.
I asked him when he planned to fly from my door;
He looked at me, laughed and then said, "Nevermore!"

The Sins of the Streets

The sins of men are seen again
Past time of the setting sun.
They appear and fight in the dark of night,
Leaving proof of damage done.

Vigilantes all receive the call,
As they plot their acts of war.
Not a blessed soul can exert control;
On the streets, the lawless roar.

They are all concealed — they are unrevealed,
And the guilty don't confess;
And it's nightly shown that the great unknown
Is the depth of senselessness.

My Only Two Faults

My wife declared I have two faults.
They're always happening.
Number *one* is I don't listen;
And *two* ..... some other thing.

Accord and Satisfaction

Principle and compromise
Rely on different things.
One will not avert its eyes;
The other clips its wings.

He who feels invincible
May see the battle lost.
One who trusts to principle
May have to bear the cost.

Those who yield and settle scores,
Accepting less than all,
Profit from the lesson more
Than those who stand and fall.

The Bloviator

"As God is my witness," he'd shout to the crowd –
The throng who had come to the hollow;
"As God is my witness," he bellowed aloud –
And more of his bluster would follow.

He claimed he believed in the power of prayer,
But no one believed what he said,
For those whom he prayed, it would shortly be shared
Had ended up worse off or dead.

His ministry clearly had forks in the road,
And some of them truly were odd,
For all his absurdities babbled and crowed —
They surely were witnessed by God.

The Moonlight Haircut

The wolfman was a person
Who concealed his nightly powers.
His barber's name was Greg, who
Would stay open evening hours.

He made it to the barbershop
By seven twenty-three:
Early evening, so to hide
his true identity.

Little did he know that night
The moon would soon appear.
The sun had set quite early,
For it was that time of year.

Suddenly the moon came out
And what surprise was Greg's!
His customer said calmly,
"Make it light around the legs."

Guardian Angel

It was my good fortune to dodge great mistakes
Because I would listen to her.
Her memorable lessons remained in my mind —
To which I could always refer.

In death, as in life, a guardian angel
Was all that she wanted to be.
The last thing she told me was that I was
Borrowing trouble if I didn't see

That yielding to influence, even from friends,
Would make me regret the unknown,
And decorous courses could not be discerned
From eyes that had not been my own.

The Traits of Time

The brightest know that all men die,
And time can never last.
We wonder why some people try
To hold onto the past.

We must accept what's newly cast
Has now become the norm;
For what we thought would always last
Could not survive the storm.

Awakenings that matter show
Horizons strange and new.
It's like the crop was gathered, though,
Before it ever grew.

It seems our days present at best
Another hill to climb.
If anything will stop and rest,
It never will be time.

The Arrival

He arrived at night, when the stars were bright,
On the day of Pentecost,

And it was his fate that they'd celebrate
For a joy no longer lost;

He would not do much, but a simple touch
Would attain him great renown;

His emphatic cries would achieve surprise,
For he weighed just seven pounds.

The Veteran

Photo by Alexander Andrews

Enduring the battle each morning,
He prayed for the silence of night.
Surviving the loss of his comrades,
He lived through the end of the fight.

His face was a portrait of gratitude
For making it to a new day.
What helped him go on was his attitude;
Experience showed him the way.

His love for the many who didn't return
Was an honor he bore without shame.
He remembered them now, with all of them learned —
By rank and by age and by name.

An Ordinary Day

She yearned to once again have just an ordinary day —
Another safe return soon after she had lost her way.

She'd run a rapid race, and had been quickly forced to move it.
She'd learned her lesson well, and could exhibit scars to prove it.

But coming home was challenging, with several tasks anew;
Recapturing lost time had left her many things to do.

She started forward slowly, and her mind was filled with doubt;
For now she lacked resources, and would learn to do without.

She made decisions soon enough, though none of them were sure —
All part of growing older, for she now was more mature.

She learned there was no black and white, but many shades of gray,
And truly no such thing as just an ordinary day.

The Address

The third week of November, many people came to see
A cemetery dedication there among the trees.

The great man Edward Everett — from Massachusetts came;
His oratory skills had earned him great repute and fame.

And from the nation's capital the President arrived,
Who'd prove he could explain as well as any man alive

What being an American had truly always meant –
In ten short sentences that only heaven could have sent.

Sunday School

I took my boy to Sunday School;
I hoped that he'd behave,
And soon he liked his teacher there –
Her lessons made him rave.

He told me we descended
From some ancient family lines:
'Cause **"Solomon had several wives
And many porcupines."**

Perenniel Questions

The bridge between judgment and intellect
Is often not easy to find.
While all of us thrive where they intersect,
They fight for control of the mind.

Knowledge is something that only is earned
By study and careful reflection.
None of it matters unless it is learned
And buttressed by strong recollection.

Both play a role in the brightest and best,
But brilliant men frequently fall;
When we examine what makes for success,
It's courage that counts most of all.

Bovine Bewilderment

The farmer tried to milk the bull;
The bull was not amused.
As for the weary farmer,
He was udderly confused.

Unsaid and Undone

There are so many things I wish I'd said
To people I cherished who now are dead;
So easy it would have been to say
What's fixed in my mind to the present day.

And so many deeds I should have done,
Except for the races I chose to run.
A number of chances I did not take,
For fear of success I would never make.

The miles never traveled, the people not met,
Producing a life of unending regret,
The one thing impairing the sleep of most men —
Decisions that can't be considered again.

Choices

We live by making choices;
We make them every day.
A few of them are black and white,
But most are very gray.

It isn't easy to predict
What we should always do,
For all of us make errors,
And some make quite a few.

We cannot turn the clock back,
For time is not our friend;
There is no way of asking time
To let us choose again.

So make selections bravely,
With courage in your voice,
And pray that God will help you,
If you regret your choice.

In and Out with Halley's

Arrived with Halley's Comet,
In 1835,
He learned to know the river well
As any boy alive.

It happened in the Civil War
That he began to write;
He left behind Missouri,
And did not join the fight.

He later moved to Hartford,
And wrote some books to sell:
"Adventures of Tom Sawyer,"
And other works as well.

Samuel Langhorne Clemens;
That was his given name,
But as a man of letters,
We knew him as Mark Twain.

In 1910 the comet —
Again would grace the sky,
And sure enough, compel him
To tell the world goodbye.

Old MacDonald had a ....

So why did Old MacDonald
Once run a family farm?
Neighbors had no knowledge what
Took place inside the barn.

Mrs. Old MacDonald hid
The family business there.
MacDonald plowed the fields while
She just kept a secret lair.

Her laborers were female;
Her clients all were men.
They'd say they wanted brussel
Sprouts, and go inside the den.

The sheep and cows and horses
Outside made their beastly sounds,
While Mrs. M's bordello
Kept its secrets from the town.

The Financier

You could not ignore, it was peril for
This man of great renown;
He'd begin to shake, and his stomach ached
When he saw Dow Jones was down.

It was local lore, that he'd grown up poor,
On the wrong side of the town,
But he did research, and he prayed in church
When he saw Dow Jones was down.

This financial sage, lived a ripe old age,
'Til the leaves had withered brown;
He would long abide, but he finally died
When he saw Dow Jones was down.

Opposing Fire

He stood there on the poop deck,
Barking orders at the crew;
The enemy was closing in,
But he knew what to do.

The captain, who was strong and brave,
Left nothing there to chance;
But cannon balls whizzed by so close,
It made him soil his pants.

Returning fire, now his crew
Earned such historic fame,
And made the Captain realize how
The poop deck got its name.

The Monkey Trial

Henry Louis Mencken was a journalist we'd see
Reporting on the "Monkey Trial" in Dayton, Tennessee.

To challenge all religion, he had done his own research,
He satirized the primates of the jungles and the church.

He wrote about buffooneries of Bible family scions,
Accounting for hypocricies of William Jennings Bryan.

The verdict showed injustice, and the law was quite surreal.
We read it in his paper, which had paid for the appeal.

If Longfellow had Written
"Little Red Riding Hood"

Listen my children – you really should
Hear the story of Little Red Riding Hood,
Her grandmother, wanting a visit real,
Regrettably served as a predator's meal.

The wolf had a big ugly animal's nose,
He thought he could hide in the old woman's clothes.
He planned to attack – the child wasn't alert;
He thought she would make quite a tasty dessert.

The only thing saving the small child from death
Was the fact that the wolf had such God-awful breath.
She gave him a bottle of cold Listerine; ®
T'was something the animal never had seen.

The wolf drank it down, never knowing what was
Its alcohol content, which gave him a buzz.
The girl escaped, hearing a snore and a cough
From the critter in bed who was sleeping it off.

Flower Child

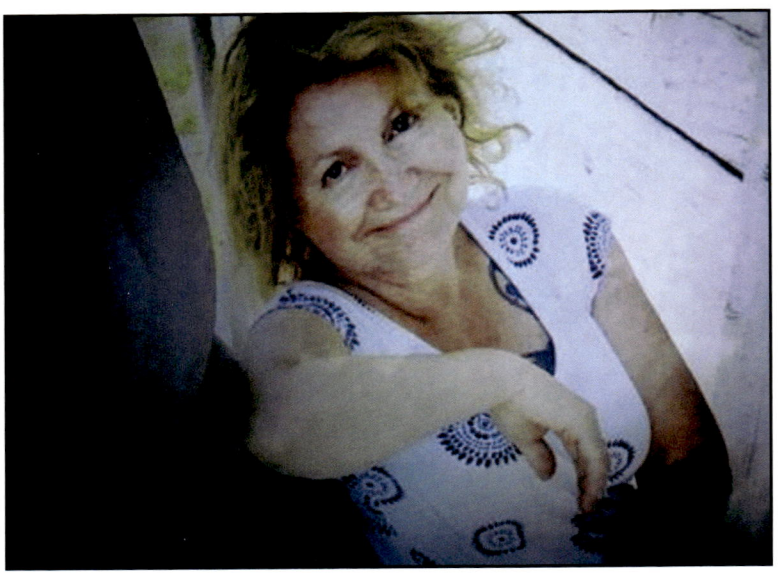

She couldn't escape her Bohemian self,
That served her for so many years.
A spiritual journey she'd never regret
Had held both elation and tears.

She recognized rapture in corners of life,
Perceiving the good in each day,
And stood by the lives who could claim no one else —
An ally in times that were gray.

Lovers of wanderlust envied her faith,
Embracing the young and the old,
Confronting each test with a smile on her face,
Concealing the scars in her soul.

No Time to Rest

He always had some four or five
Appointments in a day.
He paid his bills when they arrived,
And had no debts to pay.

He'd read a book without a stop,
And never did say why;
He never missed a photo op
Before it passed him by.

He cleaned his plate – each crumb of bread;
He never left a bite.
He'd meet his deadlines days ahead,
By working late at night.

He did not take vacation time,
And never did say why.
When asked to just relax, he said,
"I'll do that when I die."

The Best of Men

We never had him figured out; he was a mystery.
His talents were, without a doubt, amazing things to see.

And wit – his sense of humor was a privilege to behold;
He left us laughing often from the stories that he told.

He also had a talent that you saw but never heard;
He was the finest listener, and he did not miss a word.

And when he died his friends and family put it perfect when
They said he was among the best of good and gracious men.

What Matters Most

There was once a time, that we were defined
By the things we say and do.
Now the things we own, show how much we've grown,
And supplant what matters true.

Is it all a dream, does it reign supreme
That what counts is moneyed proof?
Do we longer care well enough to share?
Have our hearts become aloof?

Men and women wise, they will much despise
What now holds us in repute.
But they try to cope, and they hold out hope –
Loving others will bear fruit.

The Jury

It's said that when we leave the earth, each one of us receive –
A heavenly home if we have made the grade.
We hope that in the afterlife we all have earned reprieve –
From people that we may have stopped to aid.

The jurors know we did not always heed the golden rule,
And very, very few of us were driven
To love our neighbors as ourselves – at times appearing cruel;
We pray that they forgive the unforgiven.

Now if the verdict's favorable, and we can join the just,
Our days will be eternal without worry.
We then will all be thankful for the lessons that we trust
That we'll remember when we're on the jury.

The Avenue of Ambition

It was what she learned each day
That impelled her on her way,
But success was not an instant, lasting state;

The road was never level;
Her life was still disheveled;
There were obstacles to face and then abate.

Moving on without delay,
Keeping doubts and fears at bay,
Were the only things her conscience let her do.

She refused the act of being
Just a prisoner to fleeing;
"Run away" was not a choice she ever knew.

She had learned to live by will,
Not by ever sitting still,
And she'd only stop when someone was in need.

If the steepest prices paid
Were the dollars never made,
Then she traded them for more distinctive deeds.

Criticism

People fail most every day,
We frequently are told;
Obstacles not overcome
May leave us in the cold.

We don't need much reminding
Of the things we cannot do.
Is it not enough for us
To learn those tasks anew?

Some folks never hesitate
To chastise and upbraid —
Favor us with free advice –
Worth every cent we paid.

Wildflower Witnesses

He gathered some flowers for Minnie to press
In a book as she always would do.
He told her, "I picked them outside in a field
Where men died for me and for you."

These words may have seemed like ones better not said
By fathers to daughters so young,
But Minnie had asked about sounds from the church
Where funeral bells had been rung.

Her father, the general who loved her so much,
Would never deny her the proof
That war among men is a God-awful hell –
And wild flowers know the whole truth.

Regrets

More than a few people swear that they've lived
Their lives without any regrets.
Are they all cowards, or liars, or worse,
Or maybe just hedging their bets?

All of us think about turning the hands
Of the clock back to days of before;
No one alive can look back at his life,
And say he could not have done more.

Women and men get but one life to live;
They say they do all they can do.
But those who are honest, at least with themselves,
Confess that their words aren't true.

Learning from Mistakes

Knowledge comes from evolution –
Trial and error too.
Some will learn the right solution;
Others have no clue.

"History won't repeat itself,"
The great Mark Twain once said,
"But often times it rhymes," he felt,
Much to the people's dread.

Subdue your doubt with daring —
If you should get the chance.
All wisdom comes from sharing —
And lucky circumstance.

No Trouble at All

He suffered through the hard times,
And gotten through a war;
He lived through a pandemic
And challenges before.

He braved the darkest jungle,
And even snared a viper;
You'd think he might have some idea
Of how to change a diaper.

His wife asked him to stay at
Home to watch their little boy.
He broke two jars of baby food,
And stepped on seven toys.

Mastering the baby wipes
Took him about an hour,
He spilled the baby powder
Like he'd dropped a bag of flour.

His wife got home at night, when
He had put the child to bed.
She asked him, "Any problems?"
"There were none at all," he said.

How We Get There

History sometimes provides opportunity quite unexpected at first –
Taking what matters right into its hands; halting what might
have been worse.

Exposing us all to such men who appear malicious
or lacking in couth,
History typically wins in the end – Finally airing the truth.

Events often show that we don't have the hours to master the
job from the start,
But plenty of time then to do the job over – After it's fallen apart.

The Neighborhood Joker

The humorist was funny —
He was known most every place;
The problem was his humor
Would reflect the poorest taste.

He often would approach the
Older ladies on the block.
He'd tell his tasteless jokes to
Them to see if they'd be shocked.

They looked so very stern-faced
When they listened to his gaffes,
But then these proper ladies
Just could not contain their laughs.

The Little Things

It makes no sense to dream big Dreams –
Just take things as they come.
You cannot shape events it seems;
They march to their own drums.

Men who live their dreams are all
Exceptions to the rule;
Born to privilege, large and small
Or maybe they are fools.

The best things in our lives we know
Are never really "free";
For that's what claims of men may show –
Not what they truly see.

But those who are most happy – they
May never dream at all.
Their best things found along the way
Are often very small.

Dream Road

She was lost on the highway to nowhere
There wasn't an exit, it seemed;
She cried and she churned,
She tossed and she turned,
And couldn't awake from her dream.

It seemed all too real to her conscience;
She lived in each moment, she found.
Decisions she'd made,
She could not evade –
She prayed for a safe turnaround.

In front of her then shone a brightness
Her reveries would not encumber;
Her eyes at last drawn
To light of the dawn,
Aroused her from hours of slumber.

April 14, 1912

The night they knew was transient, and yet it seemed so daunting;
The emptiness of light and sound – the stillness was so haunting.

The ocean seemed as endless as the moonlight's long reflection;
To press on swiftly through the night was Captain Smith's direction.

When crisis came the captain's first response showed little thinking;
The last thing he expected was the ship would soon be sinking.

The lifeboats were inadequate and all too few in number;
Men and women, young and old were plunged to final slumber.

Every error men could make was made before the panic
Was claiming over fifteen hundred souls on the Titanic.

If William Blake had Written "Baa Baa Blacksheep"

Baa Baa Blacksheep burning bright,
With your coat as dark as night;
Give me some – don't make me nag;
I could use at least three bags.

First my master asked for one,
And my dame won't be outdone;
Then this boy right down the lane
Thinks your wool will help him gain

Warmth at night when it gets cold,
With its color true and bold.
Baa Baa Blacksheep burning bright –
I'm so glad your coat's not white.

Conscripts of Privilege

The Harvard-Yale Regatta, held despite the Civil War –
The crew teams raced in Worcester in July of '64.

With other young men joining Union regiments and corps,
Crewmen hired substitutes, and held onto their oars.

A mere three hundred dollars was the money that it cost
To stay there on the varsity, while braver lives were lost.

Asked years later where they fought in 1864,
They answered "Lake Quinsigamond – for trophies, like before."

The High School Reunion

Their fiftieth high school reunion was due,
To bring them to town once again.
Some laughed when they thought of the once long-haired boys,
Who'd show up as balding old men.

The anticipation to visit with friends,
Who'd been out of touch now forever,
Made some get their hair done and others lose weight,
To look good when they got together.

But when the big day had arrived for the class,
A sudden gloom hit like a wave,
It struck when they saw who did not come to town –
The classmates who'd gone to their grave.

While some had succeeded, and others had not,
And some were quite self-satisfied,
The members who most would remain in their hearts,
Were those that they learned who had died.

Balderdash

The biggest nincompoops you meet
All try to be profound.
They put on airs and think their feet
Don't ever touch the ground.

Opinions offered to and fro,
They gladly share their views,
Expecting warm reactions, though
Their words say nothing new.

Standing to pontificate
With striking eloquence.
The only thing they fail to state
Is basic common sense.

Time to Heal

Each bargain that he ever could imagine,
He made with God when taking time to pray;
But prayers he offered only led him nowhere,
And taught him God just didn't work that way.

He hoped that just a little self-reflection
Would show him what would work to stem the tide.
Just knowing that what stopped him moving forward —
Was something that had hurt him deep inside.

He searched his world for anyone to help him,
And found no one to whom he could appeal.
The changes in his life would not come easy,
Until his wounds were given time to heal.

In the Vomitorium

The actress had to leave the theatre right after the play;
She hurried to the vomitorium.
She ran so rapidly she tripped, but fell not right away,
A stranger caught her – where did he come from?

The man was strong but gentle, and he was so talented;
Just like a knight astride the swiftest horse.
When asked years later where she met the man she loved and wed,
She said, "The vomitorium, of course."

A New Day

Bursts of light shone to the ground,
That prompted them to pray
That circumstances turn around,
So they could seize the day.

They'd suffered long from men not free
Of ignorance in power –
The type who'd curse society
And dominate the hour.

Now they yearned to take control
Of life events again –
No more crippled by the cold
Mistakes of other men.

Remorse

He said, "I'm sorry" many times,
But could not change the past —
Earnest cravings to atone,
But still, the die was cast.

The image in his mirror
Simply would not vanish yet;
That image of himself, it
Showed perpetual regret.

The life that he now begged to shun
Forever carried on.
Perhaps he could not face that what
He used to be was gone.

Der Führer

In the post-war mire, he would fast aspire
To seize control and power.

And on war-torn land, you might understand
How such woe could claim the hour.

It was preordained that despair would reign
While he occupied the earth.

And his code of hate would perpetuate
Until right could prove its worth.

Now the bold and strong would combat the wrong
That appealed to ignorant men.

And then no one cried when he finally died,
And the just would rule again.

Their Favorite Pastime

They gathered for drinks at the table,
To play that old family game –
The one that had sought to determine
Which one was most worthy of blame.

"If Grandpa had never left Grandma –
For street women working at night,
Our mom might have finished her schooling,
And everything would have been right."

"But what about Dad's Cousin Albert,
Who signed up and joined the Marines?
He hoped to acquire great job skills,
But spent his time cleaning latrines."

"And don't forget Aunt Isabella
Who won the big sweepstakes one year;
She lost all her dough, when old Uncle Joe
Just spent it all purchasing beer."

And that's how they daily would gather,
And always at seven o'clock;
If ever a kind word were spoken,
It left every person in shock.

The Reckoning

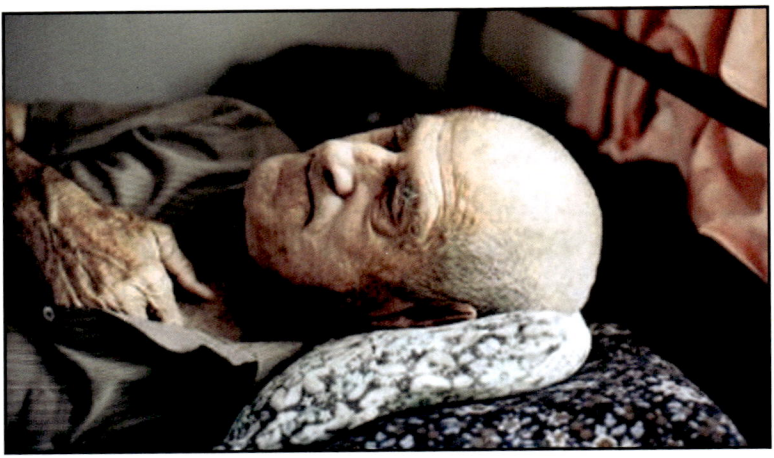

He lay there near the end of day;
They asked him plainly what he felt.
He did not know quite what to say;
He'd played the cards that he'd been dealt.

Now, might he once have offered more?
He felt that he had given much.
His talents were the stuff of lore,
Until the day he lost his touch.

He spent time with his conscience there;
The reckoning was clear and tough.
He'd once thought it was well he fared,
And yet it wasn't good enough.

He'd never taken time to dream,
Like men who lived in decades past.
He'd fallen short, or so it seemed;
He closed his eyes, and breathed his last.

Oblivion

Be wary of the tyranny of ignorance;
It's aided by complicity of all.
Nurtured by a habit of indifference,
The uninformed will ultimately fall.

Fear of change is sadly so enduring,
'Til the day of setback is at hand.
Obstinacy isn't reassuring;
Something that we're loath to understand.

Tempting as it is to love a joker,
Learning daily shall alone prevail.
Unreceptive men are mediocre —
Living missions preordained to fail.

The Song of the Gourmet

By the stagnant urban river,
Near the brown polluted water,
Stood the tavern of Batino.
Lousy food served at Batino's –
Thank God for the happy hour.
In, one day, there walked a youngster,
Looking for some new employment;
Said his name was Hiawatha –
Recent culinary dropout;
Never got his chef's diploma.

So, they showed him to the kitchen,
Where he whipped up new selections;
Not exactly standard bar fare –
Wild rice, beans and avocado,
Turkey breast on tasty frybread.
Soon the bar was gaining notice,
People showed up for the menu,
Got reviewed by local papers;
All enjoyed the native dishes
Served 'til closing at Batino's.

Suddenly young Hiawatha
Made the rounds of all the talk shows;
Featured on the Cooking Channel,
Everybody's favorite guest star,
'Til he got his own new program,
Right in Julia Child's old time slot.
Meanwhile at Batino's Tavern,
Hiawatha left its employ,
Back to lousy dogs and burgers,
Thanking God for happy hour.

Honors After Life

Frequently love is an honor bestowed,
And often bestowed on the dead.
Praise when alive, as all of us know,
Might never have cause to be said.

Selfish men may be disliked or, at least,
Not truly admired when living.
The same men may at a post-funeral feast
Be lauded with words quite forgiving.

Wretched examples are sometimes despised
By people all over the earth,
But when they are gone, you may soon be surprised
To hear just how much they were worth.

Beethoven

Born in Bonn one star-filled night,
Into darkness came his light,
And earth would know
That soon would grow
A genius and a prodigy.

His pledge became a mission now,
His mission then became a vow,
It was not fate
That he'd create
A masterpiece of symphony.

Engrafting words to melody,
His talent shone so zealously,
And would deploy
An ode to joy –
The music of the century.

The Charge of the Credit Cards

Half a small,
Half a small,
Half a small fortune.
Into the valley of Debt –
Went a few hundred.
"Forward, with little dread!
Charge to the card!" I said:
Caught in the valley of Debt
Cost several hundred.

Forward the charge I made;
Was every vendor paid?
Who'd ever pay the bill?
I hadn't wondered.
Nor did I make reply,
I never reasoned why,
Who ever cared? Not I:
Trapped in the valley of Debt
Quite a few hundred.

Sales to the right of me,
Bargains to the left of me,
Deals there in front of me;
Interest and late fees.
Much rather buy than sell,
Boldly I bought pell-mell,
Mortgage the future well.
Into the jaws of Debt,
I figured, "What the Hell?"
All that I spent, it was
Thousands and hundreds.

Alfred, Lord Tennyson
Paid cash for all he'd done;
He wouldn't mind the fun;
Nothing's been plundered.
Visa® and Mastercard® –
Getting them wasn't hard;
Merchants best be on guard.
Here come the hundreds.

Otherwise Engaged

You called to say you're sorry,
But I could not say, "That's good."
You caught me on the toilet;
But for that, I truly would.

Multi-tasking now is
Not so easy where I sit.
I'll have to call you back if
You can simply wait a bit.

You know that I forgive you,
But my words I cannot rush.
I dare not say the words, for
All you'll hear is when I flush.

If you will just be patient,
This sad chapter can be closed,
And then we can move forward
When I'm not so indisposed.

Faithful Vows

She looked into his eyes and saw
The boy that she once knew,
Who grew into a man and
Never once was less than true.

A harder working man you'd
Never have a chance to meet.
The roadmap of his life did
Not include an Easy Street.

And as his mind began to fail,
She never left his side.
The vows she'd taken years before
Would evermore abide.

So sadly destined to decline
Each year that he survived,
He wouldn't be forgotten
As a man once so alive.

Ball's Bluff

Minie balls whistled and slid through the air —
Targeting bluecoats, who fell everywhere,

Students from Harvard — men trusting, but green,
Witnessing horror they never had seen,

Forced to learn lessons they never had learned;
Home was a dream to which few would return.

For those who survived, and for all those who fell,
The place had in no way been better than hell.

Earnings of the Day

A course of trial and error, and
Then paying for mistakes –
Is what a man's whole life is from
The moment that he wakes.

He, sadly, works and must compete
Throughout the day, and then
Detect a version of himself
He'll recognize again.

And if he's lucky just enough,
He'll earn and circulate
A currency of gratitude
Before it is too late.

Life in the Hereafter

They laughed when they talked about heaven,
And questioned what it would be like.
Was there such a thing there as weather?
Would lightning up there ever strike?

He hoped there'd be cold beer aplenty,
Supplied there in limitless kegs.
She wondered if once in the afterlife there,
She'd have to again shave her legs.

They pondered if they could watch over us here –
Still witness the earth's living brood.
They hoped they could always see just how we looked —
If fully clothed or in the nude.

Would all of their best friends be present with them?
And family members as well?
They knew there was one they'd be missing, because
Uncle Emmett was destined for hell.

Fifty Years Ago

Fifty years ago,
I had not given in to convention;
I had not yielded to fears and insecurities;
I had not settled for second best;
I had not experienced the failures that have befallen me;
I had not walked away from chances to learn;
I had not declined the opportunity to serve;
I had not lost the friends I no longer have;
I had not passed by those I should have met;
I had not been satisfied with "good enough";
I had not tried to blend into the crowd;
I had not wasted second chances;
I had not borne the losses that scar me;
I had not forgotten how to forgive;
I had not neglected those who needed me most;
I had not stopped moving forward;
I had not made the mistakes that became my life;
I had not let you go,
And I had not run out of time –
Fifty Years Ago.

Miscellany

<u>Page #</u>: 55 **"In the Vomitorium"**:   Theater afi-
cionados know the meaning of "vomitorium";
others best check the dictionary.

Other Books by Jim

"Jim's Poems from the Heart ... and the Seat of his Pants"

"Musing and Amusing"

*100% of the Profits from the Sales of Jim's Books
are Donated to Charities for Underprivileged Children*